"I write to appease the creative hunger raging in my soul."

-emmett wheatfall

Diana,
Imagine with
me. Thank you
EW

He Sees Things

A book of poetry

By

emmett wheatfall

Reflections Publishing, Inc.
Inglewood, CA

Reflections Publishing, Inc.
P.O. Box 294
Inglewood, CA 90306
www.reflectionspublishings.net

Copyright © 2010 by emmett wheatfall

All rights reserved.
No part of this publication may be reproduced in any form or by any means, electronic, mechanical, photocopying, recording or otherwise, without the written permission of the author.

Printed in the United States of America

Cover and Interior Design by Reflections Publishing, Inc. Design Team

ISBN 978-0-98407895-0
Library of Congress Control Number: 2010931680

To my family

Karen, Felecia, Abrina, and Jonathan Wheatfall

To my friends

Brittany Nakasone and Wakefield Brewster II

With profound gratitude, thank you

Paul Vermeersch

Contents

He Sees Things

Using the tangible he reveals
the intangible with crystal clear concepts

protracted from careful observation—
intuit thought placed in concrete and

abstract context; whereby, subtle nuance
sees the light of day. People ask him why

he's so quiet; he tells them he sees things. He
cert's, just because a thing cannot be seen

doesn't mean it isn't there. Take your hand he
asks, place it with your palm facing your face,

then blow. Can you feel something brushing your
palm? Yes they always reply. But can you

see what's brushing your palm he adds. No is
what they invariably say. Like the

ascending dawn of morning light, slowly—
the intangible becomes tangible.

Using the tangible he reveals
the intangible. Why?

He sees things.

The King of Fools

I sat with geniuses
and belabored the point—
only to never again be acknowledged.

I sat with entitlement
until I lost mine—
then the entitled no longer knew me.

I sat with wisdom
not knowing I possessed none—
and Wisdom said, "Now you know."

I sat with fools
who hung on every word—
and they crowned me their king.

A Poet's Inspiration

I see falcons leap
from fallen trees that made the forest quake
without whimper.

Their loft lifts them higher and higher
upon the winsome winds my eyes cannot see;
yet, a balmy breeze brushes ever so slightly
against my brow.

The crystal clear brook is calm,
as I observe the movement of minnows
in fissures beneath the surface.

Cascading circles dissipate quickly
as I drop pebbles into the silent water—
as does my memory on occasion.

Therefore, I will wait to see falcons leap
from fallen trees that made the forest quake
without whimper.

I See Love

At the invisible moon
a wolf howls.
Infatuation? Yes!
I see love.

Hidden above the clouds
the moon peeps.
Fascination? Yes!
I see love.

Dancing.
Romancing.
A wolf—the moon?

I see love.

Blushing Venus

Neptune winked at Venus,
making Venus blush.
A flush of anger
rushed Uranus.

Solar flares lit the stars,
awakening sleeping Mars.
The moon—he whispered,
what's all the fuss?

The Sun said, be quiet.
Uranus, you settle down.
Mars, go back to sleep.

All the while,
Neptune smiled,
and Venus—blushed.

True Love

True love is something seldom seen
Like crushed blue ice and purple ice cream
Like chocolate grapes and pink olives
Like waste paper baskets filled with copper-coated dollars
Can't you see?
True love is something seldom seen

Sensibilities

Summoning my senses,
her sensibilities tease me,
softly, sweetly, discreetly.

Awakening my proclivities,
her sensibilities serenade me,
in symphonic overture.

So I solemnly swear,
with sensibilities and care, to tease
softly, sweetly, discreetly.

We—Are One

my skin color,
I did not choose it;
neither chose it me.
but we—are one.

I am black.
the sun kissed my
mother's father, and
my grandfather's mother,
and so on;
for we—are one.

the scorching sun,
it burns things. it
burned my people.
how offensive. by what
license, by what liberty;
yet we—are one.

me, I'm not angry;
because I am black.
neither because we—
are one. but because,
I did not choose it;
neither chose it me.

I am white.
the light kissed my
father's mother, and
my grandmother's father,
and so on;
for we—are one.

the light blue sky,

it lightens things. it
lightened my people.
how offensive. by what
license, by what liberty;
yet we—are one.

me, I'm not angry;
because I am white.
but because,
I did not choose it;
neither chose it me.
still, we—are one.

black, and white;
we—are one.

My Face

My face is your face, and yours is mine,
for the likeness is obvious to me.
Who are you I ask as I stare deeply
into the mirror of my own self.

I am not afraid of you because I'm
black like charcoal and the ashes of ember;
one tarnished by the heat of the blazing
sun, even that of dried basil and such.

There can be no greater love for you in
that I cherish you with such divine
reason, and reject the notion our color
in any way, shape, or fashion degrades our

blackness. A hew so fine my heart swoons
when I behold the face of my own self.

Patriot

They called him “Nigger!”
PATRIOT
They called him “Colored”
PATRIOT
They called him “Boy!”
PATRIOT
They called him “Monkey!”
PATRIOT
They called him “Tar baby!”
PATRIOT
They called him “Sambo!”
PATRIOT

Vietnam

His second tour of combat
He almost didn't come back

Why?

He stepped on a landmine
Almost lost his behind

About Vietnam?

He came home
He's never bitched or moaned

Just the other day
Much to my dismay
Somebody called him "Nigger!”

Who is he really?

PATRIOT

Whitey Wants to Go Back to the Moon
(A Tribute to Gil Scott-Heron)

In a sea of obscurity,
a black man lives in infamy,
while whitey commemorates historically,
one small step for man,
one giant step for mankind.

Marooned on his own planet,
once again whitey's back at it—
whitey wants to go back to the moon.

A black man ain't got no job,
no car,
no pot to piss in.

A black man ain't got no money,
no future,
no house to stew in.

Trapped on his own planet,
once again whitey's back at it;
only this time,
the first black president has said

we ain't going back to the moon—
we're going to mars.
And if we can't reach mars,
then we'll fall among the stars.

Rest assured Gil Scott-Heron—

Whitey ain't going back to the moon.

P.S. This time the revolution will be televised—
on T.V.,

Cable T.V.,
the Internet,
Podcast,
Facebook,
Tweeter,
My Space,
YouTube…

A Black Prince

His kingdom divided
Subjects in distress
Bread anyone?

Foreign enemies lurk
Wily the fox of foxes
Unholy grail?

Crowned is a black prince
Pauper populism
Ballots cast

Contrary saints and mystics
Pontiffs and atheists seethe
Poison darts fly

Knights, dark and of light
Feudalistic lords
Swords are drawn?

The court jesters rage
Spurious the edicts
A fowl's snare?

Prophets prophesy
Commoners listen
Restless waiting

Coffers are empty
The rich revile the poor
Justice, justice!

His people in peril
Hopelessly in hope
Crowned is a black prince

Juliet & Romeo

Juliet loved Romeo, and
Romeo, Juliet. Is this what
Shakespeare would have me to

believe? Could Shakespeare have
misplaced the verse that says
"For Whites-Only?" It all

makes sense when I stop to
think about it. Romeo
being black, with a big

prick; and Juliet, with her
milky white breasts; erect like
twin fawns longing for a

good suck. Was it Shakespeare's
intent to omit the
verse stating "For Whites-Only?"

Did he forget about
Desdemona—that White
Venetian; or Othello—that

Black Moor? The "Nigger" in
Venetian society.
Consider the racist

consternation of Iago; who
though a close friend, loathed
the sight of biracial love.

Juliet loved Romeo for
his blackness, firmness, and

his potency. Romeo
loved Juliet for her soft
tender sensibilities.
Shakespeare, be damned the verse,

penned or un-penned,
that says "For Whites-Only."

Queen of the Nile

I.

Tender teasing captures my attention,
as coquetting kisses leave treasures of
limn on my Nubian skin. Summoning

my weakened senses, perfumed spices arouse
forbidden passion—passion reserved
only for a pharaoh: and I am not—

a pharaoh.

Faint from feigning sincerity, my hands
caress the face of Cleopatra, Queen

of the Nile. I, erect in stature, with
my nature in concurrence, bemoan the
fact I love another. A slave woman,

who's whiteness is that of ivory, her
touch the silk of Persia, eyes filled with the
light of a thousand starlight's, a bosom

with breasts yet to give newborn suck. Her
shape—curvaceous, her temperament, that of
a young fawn. Femi is her name—

I love her.

II.

My Queen, fairest are you among all
women, who's words are revered, who's edicts
are of god. From this your fine bed I ask

immediate and certain relief. For
your people stand wanton, in need of your
whip—notwithstanding your iron rod. If

as the sun suddenly went black; the Queen
Cleopatra, whispers sensually
"I know of her—Femi,

the white slave girl—
Femi"

III.

You seek relief from me the Queen, your Queen
Cleopatra—
God?

What do you see in
the creature, that insect who crawls on dust

covered floors; that eats, what falls, after the
taste of my lips. Tell me my guardian,
why seek leave of my bed, it is reserved

for you—us. What can she do that your Queen
cannot? Take look to the east of our bed,
what do you see? Is it not Femi? She

sees us. She knows of us—I forbid her
leave, and she will come if I call.

Insect—her name is Insect, isn't it—
isn't it!

IV.

Come Femi. Come to your Queen O' Insect.

Wash me. Wash away the stain of him who
guards my life, my palace, my people. Bes—

who rejects the touch of his Queen for that
of a slave. Tell me. What is your secret?
Tell me. Queen Cleopatra, from a child

I have served you. Until this moment
my eyes have never beheld you. My Queen,
you truly are the fairest of all women.

I do confess Bes is my love. He is
a good man—a warrior, who honors his
Queen. His body bears the marks of his true

loyalty to you. It is I he crawls
too after battle. It is I who take
him to my bed and give him warmth and strength

so that he may preserve and protect you
from all your enemies. We do so in
the name of Cleopatra—

Queen of the Nile.

V.

Bes and Femi you have served your Queen well.
Femi, you I give to Bes, for him to
do as he wish, but will continue to serve

me, as you have served me since you were a
child. For as long as the Queen lives, you shall
live in my house. Your purpose will be to

remind me of true love. When I see you
and Bes I shall be reminded of what

true love looks like. Bes, defend me, protect

my people, and my palace. Your life I
place in my debt. For I, Cleopatra
decree it so.

Now leave me.

The Queen

While in quandary,
quietly; the queen quibbled.
Quelling quite quickly,
qualms with quips;
quashing questionable query,
from the inquisitive.

Amazon Women

Amazon women frolic in the moonlight;
nomadic tribesmen tremble at their sight.
Igniting passions of ancient primal desires,

flickering are the flames engulfing their bonfires.
Creature's cohabitating in the forestry of night;
primitive are the palpitations placating their delight.

Nakedness arouses the eroticism of tribal sensuality;
Amazon women invite tribesmen to take their virginity.
As couplets engage in the most sacred of human rites,

moaning and groaning puncture the silence of night.
Nomadic tribesmen are raptured to cosmic heights;
Amazon women satisfy their senses with orgasmic delight.

As lumens from the moon surrender to early light,
nomadic tribesmen gather in hillsides way out of sight.
Amazon women lay awake in the sighs of their bliss,

pondering mystical pleasures from their moonlight tryst.
Amazon women frolic in the moonlight…

The Sons of Sun

The sons of sun they sleep in soiled fields
of wheat and corn where blood has run. The ill,
they died with living dreams in flesh and soul,
these sons of sun and sons of slave widows.

Although the seeds of succession still grow,
the South shall never rise again we know.
So go ahead and whistle the Dixie,
and yearn old Biloxi Mississippi.

But always remember, the sons of sun
shall rise again, to live and reign in Zion.
To inherit the wind, the rain, the fire,
the manifold blessings freedom inspires.

The sons of sun await the risen one,
Jesus the Christ, Son above all the sons.

Two Angry Men

Two angry men
Stare face to face
Eye to eye
Nose to nose

Angry brutes
Men of terror
Merchants of violence
Purveyors of fear

Chairs scatter
Tables overturn
Patrons take refuge
Bets placed

Steely eyes
Internal fires rage
Blood vessels bulge
Fingers curl

Taunting shouts
Combatants circle
Fists raised
Strategy plotted

Suddenly—embrace
Riotous laughter erupts
Light blows—friendly taps
Another embrace

Tables return upright
Chairs restored
Beer swilled
Memories exchanged

Two angry men

The Gods of Men—They Fly

I see them
the gods of men—
they fly.

Titans among us mortals,
they rise, ascend, transcend,
reaching heights my mind comprehends.

These gods of men,
men of color,
mostly black, foreigners, few whites—
quick, strong, these gods of men,
talented, gifted gods among us.

These gods clothe themselves
in multi-colored apparel,
vivid in human imagination,
sleeveless, knee-less, and light,
fashioned from the finest of linen.

The gods are numbered for distinction,
as if they need to be distinct.
It's not for them, but for us,
so we'll know their position, role, their status,
the who's who among them.

We look at them and learn:
their moves, their styles, and their proclivities.
They are gods—these gods of men,
reminiscent of Greek gods—gods from antiquity.

Mortals worship them, but I don't.
Worshipping these gods is foolishness,
for they take no thought of me.
I watch them, but seldom if ever do I pay;

their congregations do that, I need not.

I wait until they appear on my television,
for this mortal cannot afford the price of audience.
My television is just fine, it provides instant replay;
that's why I can say:
"I saw them,"
the gods of men—they fly.

These gods do not wear robes.
They bounce, toss, and propel a ball.
Their accuracy and consistency is not of this world.
Remember JORDAN?
He is the god of all the gods.

These gods run, jump, levitate, and fly.
Limitless is the length of their flying,
for only a god can fly.
That's why I sit, I recline, I dream.
I am mortal—mere man.

I love the mystical nature of their gifting.
I imagine being one of them, but for naught—
I am mortal, they are gods.
Why? I cannot fly.
I cannot rise, ascend, transcend.
I am, and will forever be—mortal.

I see them,
the gods of men—
they fly.

There Stood I...

There stood I
Upon some leaves
When the branch above
Released a leaf
Oh the beauty of its fall
Enchanting wonder
I do recall

Uninhibited its descent
Gazing upward
I pondered what it meant
Vivid imagery, lively
Inquisitive the nature
Of my inquiry

Its color – a tarnished brown
Seasonal change saith
It must come down
Leaves below lie in wait
Wasting away with no escape

Jackie died
At thirty-three
When the branch above
Released her leaf
Oh the sadness from her fall
Absolute bewilderment
I do recall

Perplexing her descent
Like many
I pondered what it meant

Silent, certainly deadly
HIV was my sister
HIV became Jackie

Her color - a tarnished brown
The angel of death saith
She must come down
Leaves below lie in wait
Wasting away with no escape

There stood I
Upon some leaves

Fly O' Sparrow

In thorny thicket is lifeless sparrow
Never again to fly the morrow
Tiny birds—they grieve on the fencerow
A sparrow's death portends such sorrow

Dead sparrows were born to die below
The living—they circle high and low
Hymns are sung in the sparrow's shadow
Fly O' sparrow to heaven's hollow

Fly O' sparrow
Fly

In the Valley of Peace

In the valley of peace
are the dead.
Dandelions bloom
where the deceased rest;
and freshly cut daffodils lay

decaying.

When gravestones darken the sun,
the shadows rise.

Some say the dead whisper,
on certain days.

I wouldn't know,
I don't frequent then

Graves point northward.
Believers wait for redemption;
atheists sleep.
The Undertaker,
he doesn't sleep—
where sunlight fades
in the valley of peace.

His grave readied,
where dandelions bloom,
and freshly cut daffodils lay

decaying.

But Those Eyes

A woman of substance is Daisy with her
apricot colored skin, her voice the whisper
of leaves rustling in Southern wind—much
to the chagrin of black women living on the
Westside. Daisy's mane, dark like the pitch

of moonless midnight, rosy-red lips so
inviting even her indolence in light of day
incites intense lust. Daisy bares a silhouette
so alluring that white men peering out of the
barbershop window howl loudly as she

seductively strolls by with a stride so smooth
the city bus driver mistakenly stop's to pick
her up.

But those eyes—

sparkling like freshly cut diamonds mounted
behind a light blue veneer that exposes the
sensuous side of her soul. Every now and then

the window washers washing dirty windows
adjacent to 105th Street will get a wink, only
these blue collar workers reply with whistles,
much to the consternation of old black woman
selling fruit in the parking lot north of the

bingo parlor. Daisy's figure, with its curvaceous
shape, reminiscent of speed bumps lining
neighborhood streets that slow cars traveling
in excess of the speed limit, brings to mind
what every man feels when he sees a women

he wants to give a ride. Such bumps on the
street could never feel that good.

But those eyes—

always looking but never seeing. It's as if Daisy's
steely vision never fades. Piercing is the power
of her stare, humbling the morality of good

character men. Why, even the ministers and
imams struggle to maintain purity of mind and
spirit. If not for the force of soul, there goes the
grace to forget the thoughts of a romantic
interlude with Daisy. But, she's not buying it, she

knows they want her. Daisy's purse, slung over
her right shoulder accents her hips.

But those eyes—

they make lame men try to limp, blind
men swear they can see, impotent men believe
they can rise again. Of course, the fallacy of such
is certainly notable.

But those eyes—

But those eyes.

We Tango

The landlady lingers lustfully
at my door. She's certain

I want her—I do; but I don't.
She seeks to relieve me

of my virginity, and I, the key
to keeping my door locked.

So—we tango.

Alluring is the scent of her
apple-plum perfume. My

impatience inarguably releases
the pheromones of musk.

So—we tango.

We tango until the landlady has
my virginity, and I, the key to

keeping my door locked. But now,
I never lock my door.

So—we tango.

Only You

Only you.

Only you can nudge the northern lights,
make sleepy clouds whisper good night.
Force winter winds to ebb and flow,
kiss weeping willows in yesterday's glow.

Only you.

Only you.

Mandolin Lady

Mandolin lady
Strum me a song
Mandolin lady
String me along

Can we tango?
Salsa too
Dance a foxtrot
Me and you

Let's cha-cha
Samba too
Dance a waltz
Just us two

Mandolin lady

Strum me a song

Mandolin lady

String me along

The Music Sure Sounds Nice

Soulful sounds serenade the promenade
as the holiday season ends and the New Year begins.
No more Christmas carols looping airwaves, elevators, and
this here shopping mall.

How wonderful it is to hear old school tunes like:
"Kiss And Say Goodbye" by the Chi Lites, The Staple Singers
"I'll Take You There", and Aretha Franklin's
"Bridge Over Troubled Water."

My, my, my—the music sure sounds nice.

Sometimes, after momentarily peering into store windows
courting couples, arm in arm, occasionally hand in hand, pass
by.
Strolling the promenade, young mothers push baby bassinets
while punks plot their next mayhem. I'm not scared though;
mall security is everywhere.

Just look at all the foot traffic.
It's not so bad here,
I think?

Gee! How living has passed me by.
Still, I know way more than these shoppers and gazers.
What do they know about life, aches and pain, memory loss,
retirement, war, or even dying for that matter?

My, my, my—the music sure sounds nice.

I wonder , where has all the great music gone? Kids today,
know nothing about great music. My father's generation,
listened to really, really classy crooners like
Frank Sinatra, Tony Bennett, and the ageless wonder—

Mr. Nat King Cole. Young cats today try their best at crooning,
but it isn't the same. What a shame.

Look! That little baby boy is trying to dance,
bouncing up and down like that. What a juvenile smile.
Everyone's just egging him on. I see a little Sammy Davis Jr.
in him. Do your thing little boy, do your thing.

My, my, my—the music sure sounds nice.

I Only Dream At Night

I only dream at night,
when the clock strikes twelve,
when sirens whine and,
cop cars spin their colored lights;
when gunshots pierce my dreams
like bells ringing in St. Michael's Cathedral.
The noise doesn't wake me.

Crawling across my body is a spider.
I feel nothing. It bites me. I feel nothing.
Suddenly, flashing outside my window
fire trucks spin their lights.
It's my neighbor's house—it's on fire.
Where is my robe? Where is my robe!
Something bit me.

My brother-in-law Tim acts like a twit
whenever I visit my sister and niece.
I need a place to stay because of the fire.
My sister said yes, but he says no.
My mother, she lets me stay with her;
but insists on talking, even though she knows
I only dream at night.

This bed I'm in is not mine,
it's different; I can't sleep.
So I rise and go out into the dark.
Something is moving out here.
I know I am a man, but I'm scared.
I'm running, and running I stumble.
Looking back I see it's gaining on me.
I awake. It's morning, for

I only dream at night.

I'm Falling

Edge
On the edge
Knees tense, fists clinch, edge
Arms extend, lean, lean forward
Leaning forward, I fall

Falling
I'm falling
Falling and falling I fall
Turning and twisting, tumbling
I continue falling

Air
I hear air
Rushing air, rumbling air
Loud, whooshing, windily sound
Tossing, spinning, falling

SPLASH

Who Can Save Me?

Condensation settles on the windshield,
obscuring the view of things ahead as
the highway spirals in concentric circles,
leading nowhere,
but to the place
from which
my daily journey begins.

It's difficult to see,
as the headaches grow stronger
with throbbing,
the likes of African drums beating into the night,
and by towering fires,
with dancers shouting unintelligible sounds
that are incessantly annoying.

To move forward
is like trampling through a muddy marsh,
only to become entangled in hidden vines,
that wrap themselves around my legs,
binding me to the inescapable
damp and murky
landscape.

Freeing myself,
I continually stumble in areas
where the quicksand has,
but one purpose, and that is,
to swallow me whole.

I fight to free myself
from its gravitational pull.
My efforts seem fruitless
and exhausting,

sapping and depriving me
of the strength I need to go on,
to live,
to be free.

Instead of feeling lifted,
I feel immense pressure,
in much the same way
a slab of rock feels when
placed on one's chest.

I can't breathe.
Realizing for the first time
how precious it is to breathe,
I plead for a paper-bag,
but there is none,
much to my dismay
and volatile temperament.

So I hide,
in the vast oasis of me,
harboring fears
that box me into a closet
I know to be my house.
When the doorbell rings,
I refuse to answer,
for it is,
in my mind,
that I hear it ring.
I'm certain.

Who can save me from myself?
Who can reach in the toilet,
and retrieve the hairbrush
I let slip out of my hand,
that now clogs
the only place palpable
to discard the waste

clogging my soul.

Who can save me?
For I cannot save myself.

Wild Mulberries

Drunk?
I'm not—really.
Really, I'm not.
I do see Canaries!

I see Canaries
pecking at wild mulberries.
Their cheeks and beaks
stained with froth and berry.

I swear!
I do see Canaries.
A tad bit drunk from
sipping wild mulberries.

I'm not drunk!
I see Canaries!
I do—really.
I do.

Marshmallows

My watery lips and mouth they wait,
To taste the treat the heat will make.
In fire and flame that light the night,
O' marshmallows you smell so nice.

To see the sight in children's eyes,
I like how high the flames do rise.
A piece of wood to fire I'll add,
The more the merry I'll be glad.

O' marshmallows you smell so nice.

I'm A Coffee Cup

I'm a coffee cup.
Sheik to the sippers sitting in this gourmet coffee shop.
Them prudes don't think I know much,
But I know a lot.
The one thing I do know,
My job is to keep their latte hot.
Especially while they talk,
And boy do they talk a lot.

Coffee cups are multi colored too.
We come in red, yellow, green, or blue.
You thinking what I'm thinking?
Yeah, yeah, yeah, I'm white boo.
How come only white cups will do?
That ain't right;
Go figure,
Heck I'll say it,
Better us than them paper figamajiggers.

All I do is sit and listen.
If you ain't no coffee cup,
You don't know what your missin.
You ought to hear the lies money and privilege tell,
It's awfully clear they all going to hell.

After a sip or two,
By the who's who;
You'll know it's true.
Don't get it twisted,
I listen to a lot of preachers too.

Let me share with you something I can't stand,
It's a loud mouth woman with an unsteady hand.
She always finds a way to tip me over,

Spilling her latte on napkins, purses, herself and others.
You know what?
There I lay tilted to one side,
Thanking God I don't have to listen to another one of her lies.

Finally, you know what I'm about to say.
Twenty times a day I'm washed and put away.
I'm ceramic so I can take the heat.
Always stacked and racked for another command repeat.
At the end of the day I'm really beat.
So the last thing I do before the lights go out,
I tell all the other coffee cups what them sippers talked about.

I'm a coffee cup,
Sheik to the sippers sitting in this gourmet coffee shop.
Them prudes don't think I know much,
But I know a lot.
The one thing I do know,
My job is to keep their latte hot.
Especially while they talk,
And boy do they talk a lot.

On Crests of Golden Sand

From shore to balmy coast
On cliffs and rocks it boasts
While wind and rain boist
The sea, it has a voice

The seashells sit and wait
A sound do not they make
In basking gentle breach
O' the tales seashores keep

In wash and waves that sneak
It yearns the sea to speak
On crests of golden sand
Listen earth, listen land

A Good Laugh

Listen, if you ever need a good laugh,
Just recall something funny from your past.
Because laughing I'm told,
Is really, really, good for the soul.

Especially when you're feeling down,
And the only thing you can conjure up
Is an angry looking frown.
Laugh a little – you'll come around.

Take for example little children,
Silly things just thrill them.
Sometimes they bust the proverbial gut.
Obviously they didn't learn that from us.

Besides, if you ever get sick,
Take some time and think about this;
A good laugh is like medicine,
You'll feel like you died and went to heaven.

Always try to make someone else laugh.
Again – use something funny from your past.
Listen, let yourself be laughed at,
Most people will never forget that.

Laughing is about how you feel.
It doesn't require any sort of skill.
Realistically it makes a whole lot of sense,
Laughing is just like money - when well spent.

So go ahead and have a good laugh.
Remember – just recall something funny from your past.
Cause laughing is like medicine,
You'll feel like you died and went to heaven.

Goo-Goo Gaga

A fairytale must never be told by a
fairy, for a fairy has never the

tale to tell; just the one made of fancy
fashioned in whim. The infatuation

fairy often sees fallacies and goes
goo-goo gaga over them. All the while

filling the duped fairy with false feelings
of requited love. The tale of a fairy

can be found under tables tickling the
toes of the fickle and foolish; thereby

causing a few more goo-goo's and gaga's
to erupt. Back to the tale I'm telling.

Quite funny is the tiny pheromone
fairy, feverishly fulfilling the

follies fandango fairies force upon
unwitting Spanish cads—just for the hoot of

it; thereto causing a few more goo-goo's and
gaga's to erupt. Sexy fairies love it!

They eat it up in delightful ways. Why? A
fairytale must never be told by a

fairy, for a fairy has never the
tale to tell; just the one made of fancy

fashioned in whim.

The Little Paper Boat

A steady stream flowed next to the curb,
rinsing away sediment and patches of dirt.
Simultaneously something surreal was happening,

a little paper boat was rapidly advancing.
Its mysterious voyage in no way alarmed me,
seeing it sailing simply steadied my curiosity.

After a long lingering look it began to occur to me,
its origin - the ancient Japanese art of Origami.
Obviously no captain and crew were on board,

only wind and water kept the boat moving forward.
Along the curb and over a leaf,
oh what a maneuver - what a relief.

By now the current was moving forcibly fast,
being made of paper just how long could it last.
Clearly this was a once in a lifetime voyage,

something only a few paper boats ever enjoy.
All maiden voyages are filled with danger,
something it would learn sooner than later.

For just up the way was a wide-open drain,
navigating its treachery looked futile and vain.
But providence was on the little paper boat's side,

a subtle change in wind became its new guide.
As fate would have it - even the water complied,
thus enabling the little paper boat to sail on bye.

At that very moment a great idea began brewing,
the very thought of it was somewhat amusing.
I commissioned the little paper boat the USS Origami,
and declared – Godspeed to you and wherever you journey.

A Big Blue Hat and Some Tiny What-Knots

When I travel
Which is quite a lot
I try to bring back
A big blue hat
And some tiny what-knots

With me
It's never an after-thought
My mother always wants
A big blue hat
And some tiny what-knots

Once I was shocked
I almost forgot
To bring her back
A big blue hat
And some tiny what-knots

My mother gets really, really, hot
When I tease her a lot
Saying
"I'm not gonna bring you back
A big blue hat
And some tiny what-knots"

Then there's my pet peacock
Even he took a shot
Telling me "Dummy, buy your mother
A big blue hat
And some tiny what-knots"

That's why when I pray
Knowing Sunday is Mother's Day
I'd better not forget

To bring my mother
A big blue hat
And some tiny what-knots

Happy Mother's Day, Mom!

My Feet Cannot Carry Me

My feet cannot carry me to freedom,
but my mind can. Even though my mom thinks
I'm crazy, and my dad—well, who knows; he
left us a longtime ago. Why? He loves
loose women and hypodermic needles.

Clearly his mom held him too much. And his
father—well, he too loved hypodermic
needles and loose women.

This isn't folklore.

It's times like these that make me long for some
peace of mind. In my heart I cannot bring
myself to sing, "*He's Got The Whole World In
His Hands.*" Why? I don't know what his hands look
like, where his hands are located, and why he's
not in my world.

I made a wish, when I
blew out the candle on my last birthday
cake. I wished to never again make a
wish. Why? An extinguished candle is a
forgotten wish.

My mind can take me places
my feet cannot. The last time I visited
Saturn the colors were out of this world.
On the ocean floor, the amebas look
delectable. Sitting atop the great
Mt. Pinatubo is no fairytale. My
feet cannot carry me to freedom, but my
mind can.

His Mother's Only Child

Rowing a small boat is a little boy.
He is lost.
Quite naturally, fear grips him—
for he has yet to become a man.
He is his mother's only child.

An early evening fog exacerbates the situation.
Making what matters worse, nightfall settles upon
the surface of the lake.

What once began as a childish excursion has blossomed
into an unforeseen journey. Limited visibility, nightfall,
and yes—the cold diminishes his chance for survival.

While the night lingers, his eyes fill with tears,
for he has never experienced darkness. As for loneliness,
it frightens him, as would any child.

His mother scurries along the faint shoreline. By now
she is hysterical. As fears mount neighbors join her.
Caring voices call out his name late into the night.

Lamps and flashlights illuminate the dark; bringing hope
their lumens reveal his whereabouts. The sound of crying
intensifies their calls. Someone shouts, "There he is!"
Then splashing water is heard. It's his mother,
she's in the water, ferociously wading, waist deep,
her arms flailing, stretching, and reaching.

Weeping and wailing fill the waning night,
as people shout "Oh Lord! My God!, Heaven help her!"
He sobs in his mother's arms; she peppers him with kisses.
With tears streaming down her face, she utters
"Thank you Jesus." Why?
He is,
his mother's only child.

When I Was Young

When I was young I longed for love
Gazing the heavens even the stars above
Fantasy was my fancy
Inspired by my dreams
They too did entrapped me
Captivated me
Gave new life to me
Always revealing what I was made of;
How,
When I was young I longed for love

When I was young I longed for love
Who would it be
What would it consist of
Day-dreaming was my thing
Within its grandeur I found new meaning
It helped me
Most often got the best of me
Always revealing what I was made of;
How,
When I was young I longed for love

When I was young I longed for love
Revealing were my inner thoughts
Romantic soliloquies are what they taught
Reciting them over and over again
I loved releasing the pale blue moon within
Always revealing what I was made of;
How,
When I was young I longed for love

Missy M.

Wildly soft of earthy pine
Wintry wise so deeply fine

Steely strong yet surly weak
Boldly bright but truly meek

That's you Missy M.
That's you

Clearly black and darkly brown
Pertly proud a pithy noun

Deftly smart yet humbly spry
Freshly cut with witty eyes

That's you Missy M.
That's you

Written for Ms. M. Hudson, a yet to be recognized great writer whose poetry and prose are subtle not contrived, simple yet profound. A great writer soon to be revealed for any and all to read.

God Bless You!

At the Intersection of Life—
that being the I-205 and Northeast Glisan Street Freeway
on-ramp, stands a weary looking white man, who,

when walking, walks with a slight limp—

all the while holding in his hands an unfolded sign,
brow-beaten by the sun hanging so low in the deep blue sky:

just like Clint Eastwood in Hang 'Em High, only this guy

isn't wearing a scarf around his neck, hiding the injustice
of indiscriminate men, who, given the opportunity, without
conscience,

kill, steal, and destroy. Yet, the roadside beggar petitions in
silence,
using 21st century hieroglyphics, written on a used piece of
cardboard,
scribed with ink found in a black felt pen,

obtained with the same ingenuity used to get the cardboard
box—
I guess. He lacks the look of a proud bamboo stick growing
in Asian marsh,

or the erectness of a Cuban sugarcane, even that of a fat-
faced frog
sitting on the big leaf floating in a pond.

A beggar's lack of money compels him to do strange things.

Only humans are gullible enough to think humility and
debasement of one's self

are commodities to be exchanged, as it relates to the process of begging;
better yet, the posture of such.

The New York Stock Exchange offers investors greater potential for return;
but, the beggar doesn't see it that way, knowing a dirty face,
disheveled clothes, and a poverty stricken face

will sooner than later pluck a dollar from the guilt-ridden fool
driving the beat up Volkswagen Beetle: barely running itself, spewing smoke
from an engine housed on its' back instead of the front.

The exhaust is enough to kill the most environmentally conscious beggar—
over time at least. No wonder I feel so embarrassed,
when I stand at the Intersection of Life, with a cardboard sign stating,

Need Help! Can you spare a dollar? God Bless You!

Something Wonderful

Today, I walked
among the diverse peoples
of the world.

Of all the things
I've ever done,
to me, it was—

something wonderful.

My Condolences

New York Yankees owner George Steinbrenner died this morning, according to that bastion of sports news—ESPN. It was a massive heart attack, prompting shock and mourning. He was 80 years old.

I was eating breakfast in a five star hotel in San Francisco when the breaking news broke. By then, the whole world was taking note.

Given this savvy age of technology, blogging, and instant messaging, without a doubt; for some—it was quite the reckoning:
New Yankees owner, George Steinbrenner—dead.

I hear that as an owner, he is the winner of seven World Series titles,
the most ever among professional baseball owners. No question he'll be in the hall; but, then again, that's just baseball.

My condolences to the Steinbrenner family.

Meanwhile, across town an eighty year old Chinese woman opened
and closed her eyes for the very last time. For some reason the
neither the media, or the internet media, reported, broadcast, texted, nor
tweeted the passing of her kind.

She was from Shanghai, a province of China. Having immigrated

here, the Statute of Liberty always reminded her of the freedom she
held near and dear.

For sixty years she labored in the same old dry cleaner as a seamstress. Earning minimum wage by then seemed so beneath her.
She buried a sickly husband and raised three children, of whom
two are doctors, and the other; well, he's a proctologist—go figure.

They neither visit nor do they call;
all three being rabid Yankees fans and all.
They can always be found at
Yankees games; but, then again, that's just baseball.

My condolences to the Chinese woman.

An Urgent Tweet!

Every night I'm dreaming,
something quite intriguing.
I send the following tweet:
There's peace in the Middle East!

For two millennium,
there's been no frenzied mayhem;
having lived them day by day,
in such peaceful kind of ways.

Arabs and Israeli's,
both nations praying daily;
that the whole wide world know,
they've let their bloody feud go.

I know—
I'm dreaming.

Get Down Jazz #70

The artist,
he no longer lives;
yet he does,

in oil stained canvass,
hung in effigy,
bordered by wood frame,

hewn from oak
long forgotten; even
though its' circles

hidden, mark time
and life's metre.

His musicians jam,
on piano, bass, and
saxophone. Colorful

artistry, suited
and booted, the big
bill brims offering

shadow. Negroes doing
their thing, all the
while motionless

on a canvass, in
my office, on my
wall. Even though

motionless and mute,
I feel the rhythm,
the beat—and

it's jazz man, jazz.
Holding down
that grove. It's

spiritual man,
super spiritual. My
sister, my brother!

Get down man,
get down with your
bad ass jazz.

Change

I'm all the change
I'm going to see.

Why?

The only thing
I can change—
is me.

And I'm not done yet.

A Proverbs

A crowded room
offers no privacy,
in much the same way
a no trespassing sign implies,
one more is too many. A

king size bed,
is made for only two;
however, just enough space
is available for the 2 year-old,
who'll hop in unannounced. A

couple, who occasionally
share a Root Beer Float,
should always use
separate straws—
to avoid the backwash. A

standard size door
is not designed to let
two people pass through
simultaneously. Therefore,
men should be gentlemen.

Proverbs to the wise
and wisdom for the foolish.
Each beginning with the
letter A and ending with a
period.

I Say

when a man
loves a woman,
for her beauty—
is it love?

when a woman
loves a man,
for his virtue—
is it love?

men say,
for beauty,
they give
love.

women say,
for virtue,
they give
love.

but I say,
love is beautiful,
and virtue, love—
that's what I say.

The Weight of a Book

A book is worth its weight in gold;
In print are gems the author told.

Each page is filled with sage advice;
Its myths of import do delight.

With candle lit beside the bed,
The nights are long and days have fled.

To study is good the teacher screeds,
So late at night the learned read.

The mind that learns is set to gain,
A place in life portending name.

A book is worth its weight in gold;
In print are gems the author told.

O' Ancient of Poets

Sound aloud the rendering of a new sonnet
O' ancient of poets. Bring me the treasures of
wisdom metered in the lines of verse, and mesmerize
me with words till they dance anew and slow.

Give me stanza's rolling like fields of wheat driven
back and forth by eastern winds; winds that summon
the whistling of age old mariners plotting course
on the high seas. Sound the rhetorical flourish

of words that create visions of love;
whereby, a young maiden's heart sings like a jealous
songbird. The poets all huddle in their
masses, in anxious anticipation of the

formal declaration of a new sonnet, to
be spoken by the ancient of all poets.

Poets

I don't understand
what poets say.

Wouldn't you know it?
I am one—

a poet that is.

ABOUT THE AUTHOR

emmett wheatfall is an aspiring poet. When it comes to poetry, the first letters of his first and last name are in lowercase. He says, "I lowercase the letter's "e" and "w" out of my respect for the art and craft of poetry, and in recognition of what my poetry mentor suggests I am at this time. I am an Apprentice Poet."

It was in high school where emmett first discovered his creative ability and talent. Acting in school plays became his passion. From there he went on to doing some acting in college. But it was his dramatic renderings of the famous "I Have A Dream Speech" by the late Dr. Martin Luther King Jr. that brought him notoriety.

Subsequent to that time emmett has written numerous poems as well as recorded two CD's. The first CD is entitled "When I Was Young" and the second "I Speak."

At this time emmett continues to read, write, study, and perform poetry. You may contact emmett by email at ewheatfall@gmail.com, or write to him at P.O. Box 30105, Portland, OR 97294.

What people are saying about

He Sees Things…

emmett's poems are storytelling at its finest—the reader becomes a part of his world, his thoughts and his feelings. Each word, phrase, period, comma and dash all play an important part of each and every poem. Most importantly, the reader is left with knowing more about the poet himself.

- Carolyn J. Lee, *Conference Coordinator*

… his poetry is just another aspect of his unique ability to communicate thoughts and ideas. He invokes political, spiritual, and intellectual discourse in his writings that are timely. emmett provides an excellent voice in this dialogue.

- John Garlington, *Social Activist*

LaVergne, TN USA
27 December 2010
210146LV00003B/1/P

9 780984 078950